Copyright © 2020 by Irene Koh Studio

Illustrated and design by Irene Koh
hello@irenekohstudio.com

All rights reserved. No part of this publication may be reproduced, distributed or transmitted in any form or by any means, dectronic or mechanical methods, including photocopying, scanning.

Anyone can love a
rose
but it takes a
great heart
to love a
leaf

NEVER
LOVE
IN A
HURRY

To love
is human

Love all
Trust a few
Do wrong to none

Love
is not finding someone
to live with
it is finding someone
you can't
live without

Love is not a race

Look for
the good
in love

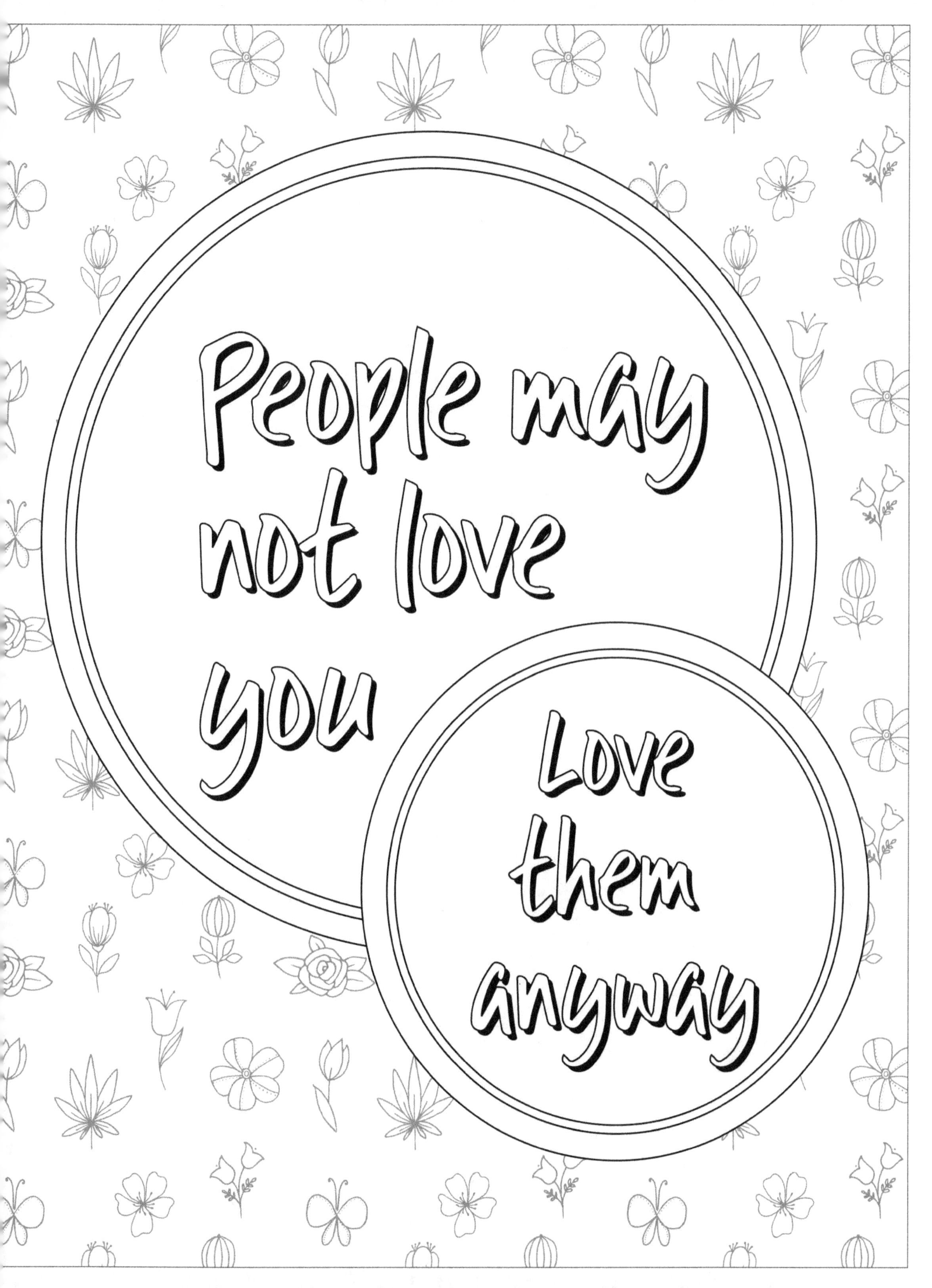

People may not love you
Love them anyway

Familiar Acts
Are
Beautiful
Through
Love

YOU
ARE
LOVED

Learn to
Love
with happiness

LOVE
IS
COURAGE

The Greatest
Gift
of all is
Love

KEEP
Love
ALIVE

LOVE WORKS

HATRED DOESN'T

HE WHO PLANT KINDNESS REAPS LOVE

LOVE
TURNS
WORK
INTO FUN

It Is Good
To Be Rich
But It Is Even Better
To Be Loved

There Is No
Perfect Love
Only
Human Love

CHOOSE YOUR
LOVE
AND LOVE YOUR CHOICE

We Don't
Love People 'Cos
They're Beautiful
They Are
Beautiful
To Us
'Cos...
We Love Them

No Burden
Is Heavy
When It Is
Carried
With Love

With Love
You Are
Never
Alone

FAITH
Makes
All
Things
Possible

LOVE
Makes All
Things Easy

If You Love Someone
Say
It
Today

www.ingramcontent.com/pod-product-compliance
Lightning Source LLC
Chambersburg PA
CBHW081458250726
48662CB00009B/3132

9 781656 997722